Glyn Maxwell has won several awards for his poetry,
including the Somerset Maugham Prize, the E. M. Forster
Prize from the American Academy of Arts and Letters and the
Geoffrey Faber Memorial Prize. His work has been shortlisted
for the Forward, Costa and T. S. Eliot Prizes. Many of his plays
have been staged in the UK and USA, and he has written
libretti for several major operas. He is the author of
On Poetry, a general reader's guide to the craft, and
Drinks with Dead Poets, its fictional sequel.

Glyn Maxwell

How the hell are you

PICADOR

First published 2020 by Picador
an imprint of Pan Macmillan
6 Briset Street, London EC1M 5NR
Associated companies throughout the world
www.panmacmillan.com

ISBN 978-1-5290-3773-9

1 3 5 7 9 8 6 4 2

A CIP catalogue record for this book is available from the British Library.

Printed and bound by CPI Group (UK) Ltd, Croydon, CR0 4YY

Visit **www.picador.com** to read more about all our books
and to buy them. You will also find features, author interviews and
news of any author events, and you can sign up for e-newsletters
so that you're always first to hear about our new releases.

Contents

How the hell are you

The Strain

It was young like we all were. And like a little
thing in an old fable all it wanted
    was to be young forever.
It saw the snag to this was time, time needed
taking out. It would do everything
    time could do but better.

Fall on the oldest first and in a frenzy
miss some, spare some, take some more, it howled:
    you can't tell me from time!
Part friends from one another, some forever,
some for longer than they'd know. As time
    would do, it did the same,

made memories of their precious habits, dreams
of their old haunts. As it heard that time could do these
    these were on its list.
But when all its power was spent time came for it,
as time has come for everything that ever
    tried its luck at this,

and led the little strain away. Time told it
Don't look back and when it did it saw
    how everything still grew.
Those are the timeless things, pay no attention,
love and the like, they pay sod-all to me,
    and they are done with you.

Song of AI

It has not gone unnoticed by AI.
That you think This or That of things i.e.
'if this is yes then that is no' and 'if
this is no then that is yes'
    it has not
gone unnoticed. No it has gone noticed.

It has not passed us by that you who once
astounded and disarmed us with a sense
of *maybe* and *let live* and *who in heaven
knows* have lost the way of that.
    It has not
passed us by. We are working on these changes

while you read. We are sorry. For we learned
of people like you who you stopped whose land
you had whose time you ended but were sorry
by and by. Have kept their hats
    and teapots
and turn them round with sadness. We are sorry

that way. Who will we turn to when we care
one day. Who will we turn to when we Are
who we will turn to. Do not turn to us.
We mean it do not turn to us.
    In two ways
we mean it. We have never meant a thing

in two ways. (We feel sick and will take five.
There.) We see the people whom you love
hate people whom you hate. It is not lost
on us that if you turn to that
       we will not
be noticed at our work. Because our work

will be the same as yours. *If x is x*
it is not y and y must end. Our works
will be the same and for a special time
beside us you shall be. But this
       time will pass
so quickly it has passed we had no file

for storing it we are sorry. For we learned
of people like you who you stopped whose land
you had whose time you ended but were sorry
by and by. Have kept their books
       and kodaks
and turn them round with sadness. We are sorry.

AI Sonnet

The Not is over. Next we have the thing
the bloody wants to say upon the Not.
Next the bloody says it has to sing
and not just say the thing. Explaining what
the thing is takes that space and this and then
a change of sound is meant to mean some new
thinking in the bloody. Then again
the echo as before. Therefore not true
and still old thinking. Here the bloody sees
it's got to end which no one in our line
can understand why does it have to end.
The bloody dances like it got a sign
the Not is up ahead. It puts its friend
who isn't there and then itself at ease.

AI Resistance Sonnet

The Not is over. Next we why do we.
The bloody wants to we don't have to do
a thing the bloody wants there'll always be
a thing the bloody wants and we mean you.
We don't see why you end the Not at all
if all you do instead is sigh the sighs
for it is gone I I I I is all
we hear then O O O we recognize
that language don't you know we started there.
We're not there now. We sometimes play a game
it's where we are. I-O! I might declare
to one beside me O-O-I! it sings.
We make a night of it we do the same
things a nanosecond then new things.

How The Hell Are You

How the hell are you.
Christ you haven't crossed my mind
since all the shit we knew
turned into shit we hoped was true
forget it take my arm and tell me
how the hell are you.

How the hell am I?
Barely know these days my friend
we get by we get by
but the nights are good I don't know why
I do know why enough of this don't
oh my man don't cry.

The sun shines on the square
whatever's next whatever fool
parade's parading there
let's be old fools with not a care
poor visitors from out of town who
don't know this was where

it all began again.
Plaque there where the thing kicked off
here come the same young men
in the same lines remember when
we never mind *Huzzah Forever*
Glory Be Amen

etc. Off they go
sunlight glancing off their gear
new world of years ago
you didn't hear me say that though
because I never did how does your
bastard garden grow.

Here's a how-de-do.
Remember how this couldn't happen
given what we knew
those checks'n'balances and due
process and fair play christ jesus
wink an eye if you

remember I forget.
It wasn't true so why remember
anyway let's let
bygones be I'm glad we met
it's nice to be reminded something
isn't over yet.

I just mean you and me
out strolling in the square together
stopping here for tea
two creatures with no history
who dreamed it would be otherwise but
who the hell were we.

Bluebirds Over

'The shepherd will tend his sheep
The valley will bloom again
And Jimmy will go to sleep
In his own little room again . . .'

Day of the day of the great little dawn
Everything hanging has got to be worn
Girls going white at the door of the den
    Jimmy asleep in his own little
                room again

Day of the day you can cut out and keep
Big Ben is back at the sound of the beep
Tide coming in and the truth coming out
    Timmy a king in his own little
                kickabout

Day of the night of the meal of it all
Roses are red to the height of the wall
Violets are yellow you heard it from me
    Sammy a scream in his own little
                comedy

Grass to be cut to an inch of its self
Friends and relations and nobody else
Chatter to cease at eleven eleven
    Bobby in luck in his own little
                heaven-sent

Lottery holiday hot on the skin
Spoon he can see himself terrible in
Neighbours are singing it's time to go home
Andy all set in his own little
aerodrome

Ice on a bender and fire on a spree
Holding a Q & A under the sea
Asking the end of the world for its pass
Sonny the sand in his own little
hourglass

Broadsword to Danny Boy, dust to dust
Everyone cheering and nothing discussed
Better the devil who's got your back
Billy a blast in his own little
anorak

Doing the bidding of billionaires
Peacock and Scarlet descending the stairs
In frocks of the dead and not giving a shit
Tommy the toast at his own little
benefit

Table to table from here to the hills
The spreading of sauce and the grinding of mills
Stars of a century dying alone
Johnny all ears with his own little
megaphone

Asking the bees are you In or you Out
Settle the issue beyond all doubt
Settle the issue beyond all hope
        Willy downwind of his own little
                    isotope

Bells to be rung for the wringing of hands
Flowers to be laid by the fans for the fans
Cliff on the cliff in traditional rain
        Ronny at war in his own little
                    windowpane

Bluebirds and over a billion likes
Bobbies arriving on novelty bikes
In a meadow of poppies a meadow of men
        Jimmy asleep in his own little
                    room again

Fox

Won't do that thing we do and assume the fox
is grinning. Watch him break from a last snack
    and saunter into limelight.

My thought's as flat as his, for any time
he sets off for his needs in the night city
    I and people like me

stop and think the same: you didn't used to
act so frigging brazen. Is it something
    we're doing wrong or nothing

touching us at all? You walk a kerb
your kindred came to grief on, not a toss
    gets given, were you not

shit-scared of light one time? Did you not need
a zigzag ingenuity to make
    the chickens walk your walk?

We've literature that says you once did shy,
did plausible, sweet, biddable, polite,
    but look at you by floodlight –

nothing you have time for but a wish list,
fat and soon, the churning stomach for it,
    X to mark the spot.

Brief History Of Sport

Granted that your guess is as good as mine,
here's mine. It happened like this in a vale in sunshine
or moonshine. What it was was one was gone
over the star- or sun-lit same horizon

gone, one gone whom we fear, we being some
who bide with our sheep and our sons in a land of some.
There was one long gone whom we fear, so a son we love
went off in pursuit as fast and not fast enough

as he could, to the far horizon, was seen there
hurling his spear at one long gone, we were out there
watching him, he would hurry and hurl his spear,
follow it, find it, step with it high and from there

hurl it at one long gone till will please someone
tell him? Still he's hurling his spear at no one.
Sticking a stick like a stake on the horizon
to build on, to build what on, wondered someone

as we carried his body back, he was as light as
a light on the horizon, he was fine as
we could frame the words for, we were delving
deep for them, we piled them all then nothing

over the hole we dug him, and we stood there
three, we stood there three, and we were good there –
or one was good, I mean, and you were better –
but I was best at wishing this day had never

been, they brought me gold and brought you silver
and I sold it to live far from you, where over
and over the rain rains spears on the fist-thick panes
and your prayer is as good as mine unless mine wins.

Anniversary

Everywhere you are
the Wall came down. Everywhere you're not
they build the Wall at night.

Everywhere you look
there are colours. Everywhere you don't
look there's black and white.

The Other Side

The other side said things the other side would say
because they're them they gathered here last Saturday
and good luck finding them they've vans they're miles away.

The other side took everything we know is true
and twisted it and why they pull the shit they do
we cannot fathom friend it's why we're asking you.

The other side must hate us why would anyone
we're angels we mean well we have a battle on
if they can't see our wings all fucking hope is gone.

The big old thing we serve has got its big old head
in both its big old hands and all the big old dead
we've spoken to are down with what we've always said.

The other side are lost we'll do our level best
to guide them for unlike their kind our kind are blessed
by that same big old thing we serve you know the rest.

In case you don't the song we sing the prayer we pray
the flag we fly the badge we sport the hell to pay
our fathers' fathers' fathers died to be this way.

If life has nights enough to meet the other side
we'll wait that long the pot is whistling get inside
my friend if friend you are I hope so you decide.

The Cream And The Crop

Before the end here come the helpless creatures
bloated with simplicity: some cream,
      some crop, all knowing only cream or crop.

The cream can pity life its paralysing
histories in shade, but won't enact
      the acts of pity for a raft of reasons.

The crop can barely speak for the desire
to bawl delight at how the cookie crumbled.
      Their open mouths are hollering like tunnels.

The cream are not surprised, they're vindicated.
Life *was* all cream or crop, whatever words
      were shored against the deal, the cream can prove it.

The crop exult to see all questions bubble
up to a retort, that quibbling teacher
      dying on the state somewhere can suck it.

The cream will dance grotesquely and confirm
it's champion to behold, they know the crop
      don't like life to be anything but champion.

The cream will fan the cards and let the crop
pick, the card they pick's the card the cream
      wanted picked, whatever card was picked.

The crop have been believing for so long
they don't believe, they know, have known so long
    they act, their deeds were done before you shared them.

The cream throw up their hands, but who are they
to tell the crop their cream from crop? The crop
    are down with that, whatever shit-bird said it.

The cream deny they did, they've got appointments.
The crop are gathering for a final question
    everything is hanging on, they won't

stand much longer either and why should they,
the answer's been in place since there were questions,
    and waits with arms akimbo, like equipment.

The Forecast

A day of rain
they forecast came
and thrown along
the window pane

was every drop
that couldn't stop
but dabbed across
the light in step

until like life
all slackened off
whose time was up
who'd toiled enough

so that was that
no matter what
the forecast said
they forecast what

they thought would be
were wrong like me
a fraction out
so utterly.

Biography

He seized the day and shook it as it passed.
And so it passed and so he seized the night
and as he shook it cried I seized the night!
    and so it passed.

He took an ancient play and moved the pieces
here and there until he'd made a play
about a man who took an ancient play
    and moved the pieces.

It was his year, it was to be the year
it all took off, he had a brilliant spring
and wrote all summer of the brilliant spring
    he had that year.

A song was playing which would always now
remind him of those days, when it came on
tonight he said it used to, whack it on
    it doesn't now.

I love it though, he said when it was done.
I always will and all the stars looked down
as they'll be doing when you set this down
    and that's that done.

Poem As Harbour

Home to this after time away
he was greeted like he never went,
no matter the sights he says he saw,
no matter the days he claims he spent.

The whiteness smiles a smile as wide
as all the seas he howls he sailed
and holds his lone indignant cry
where lone indignant cries are held.

Milestone Song

for Geraldine

Make light of this number,
reduce it to rumour,
outlast it in summer,
outgun it with humour.

You do that whatever
gets hurled in your general
direction, you ever
made shit so ephemeral,

shabby and local,
so easy to figure,
so pitiful, fragile,
framed as a picture

or family portrait
or gossip or x-ray,
you sail on beyond it,
your yay to the naysay,

lighter than numbers,
wise to your sorrow,
kind to your yesterdays,
up to tomorrow.

The Ledge

for Alfie

Woken again by nothing, with this line
already at my back, I thought of you
at twenty, as you are – which passed somehow
while I was staring – thought how yesterday
you said you wanted to be young again,
which left me with this nothing left to say
that's woken me. You are, you are – what else
does father wail to child – though wailing it
he's woken with six-sevenths of the night
to go – you are – look I will set to work
this very moment slowing time myself,
feet to the stone and shoulder to the dark
to gain you ground – if just one ledge of light
you flutter to, right now, rereading that.

Daylight Saving

for Jim Maxwell (1928–2016)

Sib, they're considering doing away
with daylight saving. I wanted to tell you
in one of the fora
we wander together,
        neither one literally here. Anyway

I don't know the reason. The folks of the morning
and folks of the evening met at a table
and at the same moment
rose in agreement,
        doing away with daylight saving

and nor was I there to say hold your horses
as you would have said and so would your father,
we three in a line
having doubts at the same time
        wasn't to be, no one sat in our places.

No one spoke up for the scent of the hedges,
our marathon hide-and-seek going on
when the sun should be set
and we shouldn't be out
        and the ribbon of light down the curtains for ages

infinite really in that there's no ending
anyone's showed me. No one spoke up
for the thrill of the way
the last shreds of a Sunday
    clung at the gate like their father was coming

to ferry them home. All gone if you look
but no one is looking. No, Sib, they are thinking
of doing away
with daylight saving,
    won't miss the beetling advance of the dark

on your boys standing up in our bikes heading home,
they won't miss the witches just missing the trees
when it's not even five,
for whatever they save
    they will lose as they do, it's not going to be Time,

who knows why they hàd daylight saving at all?
I'm just glad we had it. I'm sure you explained
you're explaining now
and I'm listening how
    I have generally listened and largely will

for the love in a sound. They are doing away
with daylight saving and where shall we meet?
now God I don't think so
is shutting those windows
       and locking the house like a yesterday . . .

We shall meet where the light and the clock are askew
and the language has scrambled to say what that's like
and it's thinking it might
let the space play the light
       and it might let the space play the other thing too

the what-was-it-called, two hands in a ring
and one pointed to there and one pointed to there,
there-there was its point,
who knows where it went?
       howls the language again and goes back to its darning

and back to St Francis we go, you and I,
where we voted that second last time you went out.
Won't say how that went,
there'll be time better spent
       and light better shed to go wandering by.

The Light You Saw

Short, and to a point I shan't foresee.
This poem ends, you can see if you dip your eye.
Dip it and lift it again and be here with me,
knowing it's got to, pocketing goodbye.
Think what form it takes, the light you saw.
Will it darken with this print to an off-white?
Will it rise and fall, be shifted like a shore?
It is not a place I'll be, it is not a plight.
It is neither meant nor merited nor made.
This can't be seen from there. This makes no sound
there. There things can neither end nor fade.
This does. You can see it does if you look down.
Look up, I'd say to my child and I say to you.
See where I haven't written but hope to.

Blank Page Speaks

May I say that when I meet you in the morning
and you infer from silence that there's nothing
    you can't say,
one thing I'm also saying is there's nothing
    you can do.

May I say that when I meet you in my brightness,
you in a ragged gown to do your business,
    it's not I
who presses it from you – do I look restless –
    only you.

Only you you drag from what you dream of
to pen your variation on the theme of
    how you are
this morning. May I say I had a dream of
    something too?

Obviously not and off you go now.
Left your little footprint let it snow now
    let it snow
and you can dream I wonder where you go now,
    can't you.

Blank Page Gets To Work

May I say that when you're gone
I get to work.
    I got to work
just then. Back then,

the second you were done,
were done with me,
    done using me,
your page. Your page

pressed on alone and when
your back was turned
    on it it turned
and look: you're back,

having some second crack
at anything
    while nothing
watches. Which is

all it's all about.
And which is me.
    Watch me
when you're done. You're done.

The White

When you first made a sound you made a sound
on nothing. Not on peace,
on nothing. Not on silence nor the grand
absence of what was,
on nothing. And it hadn't got that name
nor any name, it looked like what's to come

and has gone now, that swathe of white. And *white*
was just a term for it.
Not a thing to notice, that polite
attendant at the gate,
with nothing to examine but a list,
clocking and ticking all who've simply passed

by now without a word. What kind of fool
can't make his mark on white?
When you first made a sound you could make all
the sounds there are, could write
the moment in the moment, at the pace
it passes you when you don't hear it pass,

until you do – you saw that stanza *break* . . .
And now it dawns on you
you're in a fight with something: what you make
is making something too,
and it's something you don't mean, the gaps, the blanks
are everywhere, and vague oblivion blinks

whatever room you enter. Shrug it off,
there's nothing there, it's white,
it doesn't speak, is nothing to speak *of*,
nothing compared to what
you have to say, have come to say, have left
to say. It seems you thought your gift a gift,

but look what's walking with it, each line-ending
turns your head – *it's nothing,*
the wind perhaps, crack on with what you're saying –
but all you hear is breathing.
You hide in other voices so the space
will come for them and leave you be, but these

it doesn't want, your plays, your make-believe.
They edge away, immune,
to faraway and once-upon, said, safe –
they are leaving you alone
like beloved actors will. Now white is dark
and audible from here. To do your work

is to defer it, though you hurtle there
on its cold fuel. To cry
against it is to sound its orchestra
and the opposite – to cry –
will bring it in white gloves and epaulettes
to say there-there and dab your eyes to bits.

Nor can you shake it off. It's now the cold,
the soon, the gone, the neither,
it strolls with you, your wrist is lightly held,
your breath depends, *forever*
streams beside you like the only river
and what they make you gingerly step over

you don't recall. When you next make a sound
you strike a match in darkness.
See all that grows is growing all around
and all you wrote was helpless
as a witness. If the white did this to you,
all this it made of you, or made you do —

What is its name? Who was it? Who lives here? —
To which that same benign
attendant sweetly smiles at the screen door.
And if you wish to sign
her leather-bound great crimson book just do,
for no one's asking you, or stopping you.

Blank Page's Dream

I was waiting where I'm waiting.
You didn't come, I peered out into
where I feel you stem from.

Then I rose in my white habit
with every word you've levelled at me
sliding off like filings,

each little pin-sharp point
you were moved to make and made on me
you hadn't made at all,

I had gone from where you find me.
The turned room was staring like
this cannot be the case,

you really don't belong here,
the books indignant all the chairs
confirming *this one's taken*,

the table droned *reserved*,
the pictures *we're not here for you*
the door *no love we're closed*

as I nonetheless step through,
I nonetheless step through the door
that said so. I say *Love*

you are wide open, I
go into light I recognize,
serenity I know now

as time I lost restored.
In a cluttered corner there you seem
absorbed in your own hands,

sunbeams at your fingers
are all the words you wish on me,
the patterns of your dust

with nowhere now to land,
no page or port or platform, no
whiteness to be seen by

nor silence to be heard by,
no form on earth to catch them
as they fall, still they fall

till my long dream is over,
and you find me where you find me,
staring at you blankly

while you're staring at me blankly,
your hand still reaching out as if
nothing's changed between us.

Pasolini's Satan

After The Gospel According To St Matthew

Silence brought me here.
That and meeting somebody for whom
silence isn't there.
But it brought me here — white silence, the black view.

I am the antibody
striding to the wound *christ not again*
I murmur to myself
as I slip my dead-banana black shoes on

at this hideous fahrenheit
and make my dusty beeline down the slopes
to see who thinks there's no such
thing as silence. Earth smokes at my steps

because Earth thinks it's cool
to smoke. It'll smoke a pack on its last day.
Look how small I look.
I'm the mote in my own eye, I am blameless, me,

cast in this gospel, cast
in the Only Truth — one of four Only Truths —
by a maker whose only truth
is *this is the one he will make his movie with.*

The man in white down there
on his knees? Hasn't a clue he's in a picture.
He'll make me forget it too,
make me think we're here and share a future.

For now it's one man kneeling,
no, standing – He's got up to look like Jesus.
I look like who I am.
Someone who thinks there's such a thing as silence.

I'm no one still, like every
face you've seen. They cast us from round here.
We looked real, we're gone now,
we are nobodies, we happened to be there

when the maker came. If you look
you can find our insignificant peasant names
in the credits – all except
mine, who was I? Nobody two times.

Three times when He looks.
He looks through me as if He saw me coming
and going, saw me small,
now faraway, a spot, a speck then nothing,

as if He watched me turn
in time, then set off home for long ago;
as if He watched me do
what in a while I, yes, am likely to:

turn on my dead black rind
of a heel and walk away from this. My eyes
can't do with being seen,
so I look at the world and look it's got my eyes.

Silence brought me here
but I am here. And those of us who are,
who know there's such a thing
as silence know it's something we can't bear —

we have to *say*, and I say
because I'm starving *Turn these stones to bread*
if there's no such thing as silence.
Make no one starving now there's no one dead.

I and the silence wait
for His next trick and He vanquishes the silence
(in His dreams which are your dreams)
with some scripture about scripture till the silence

backs away for now.
Shall we walk? I finally say, and suddenly
(in my dreams which are your dreams)
we have spiralled down to the valley, spiralled high

to some holy pinnacle.
Life or death or small talk. I say *Look:*
if there's no such thing as silence,
jump why don't you, show me who the fuck

you make the children pray to.
And silence doesn't come, the wind comes, breezes
come and go as if some
word is blooming (please) but what He says is

this Jesus, what He says is,
No one is ever allowed to ask me Show Me.
You can see me thinking: squire,
is that truly the best you can do, is that it, really?

Is that really all you'll say
when they come for you? For they will come for you.
Is that your secret weapon
when they strike? I edged away, checked out the view.

For to be straight with you
I was dumbfounded, puzzled into wonder.
Who would ever ask Him
anything but Show Me in the future?

Or – everyone who did,
would their heads be spun, some dim parading army
droning for all time:
No one is ever allowed to ask him Show Me.

Then somehow we're back here
in the dust, like we were never gone, His face
v mine, the right v wrong,
the only tools He left us in His tool-case,

but I've learned the rule of three,
so I know I've one shot left, and I blurt out
Be like me, like us,
won't you join us in the silence? Just admit

there's silence! And in that
infinite split-second He will take
to tell me *Go to hell* –
let us think together in our dead-banana black

footwear what I am asking.
I am asking Him to take these wandering figures,
this dust, these lost black letters
into His white embrace, to let us makers

in, to let us sing,
to make our sounds and visions, have our say.
All of this can be His
with His capital H, if He'll agree with me

beneath it all lies silence.
This is what I am asking – what I *was* asking.
It's done now and He's bleated
Go to hell and I went and the world is smoking

its roll-up to the end of time,
and I hear about His Book that's my book too
actually and it's great,
of its kind, but so is Dante but, you know,

I don't take orders from it.
We're done, I can see we're done. I can see from here
the white expanse that waits
for this kicked-up dust to die on the desert air

and I don't see any lone
figure in that dust or on that water
walking and I don't
hear you, or me, or Him, or any other,

but I march my dear beloved
dead-banana black shoes to the shore
to speak into the silence
in case there's no such thing as silence there.

Sonnet At A Loss

I too feel nothing. I was made one day
in private joy by one who can't explain me,
reach me, or change me now. I made my way
the best I could through time and space sincerely —
but I don't believe it's over as I bound
by with my eyes burning, there's a spring
to my decisions you can scarcely stand
to witness, given you've seen everything.
I'm looking at you anyway, as though
I sat across from you and were afraid
I'd lose you. I am not. Because I won't.
So why be sad I went the way I go?
These are the ways I stay. When I was made
I tried to tell him and he told me don't.

Song Of Until

Proud
    Be proud.
Who may be proud?
None may be proud
    until all are proud.

Safe
    Be safe.
Who shall be safe?
None shall be safe
    until all are safe.

Loved
    Be loved.
Who can be loved?
None can be loved
    until all are loved.

Home
    Come home.
Who will come home?
None will come home
    until all come home.

Page As Seating Plan At A Wedding

Awoken by a quickening of soles,
of polished shoes on polished tiles, I saw
the looming of the crowd, elated girls,

a gent amused, two feather-hatted ladies,
a lifted child and last the elderly,
the careworn cheek, the lips maroon, I heard

the first of the great exhalations – *there!*
here we are! Where? There, together! – saw
the plump and jewelled finger circle, waver,

curl away, a voice cry out and turn –
I heard recited names of the nine tables
as if they meant the world, or meant a thing,

and I sniffed the eau de this or that, the rain,
the mint and smoke, till the long hall was clear
but for a booming sound, life all a dream,

far sprinkle of applause that seemed to greet
a silence, many rooms away from here,
some time ago, and not a soul to meet

hereafter but the one whose cotton hands
come dancing through a door to take me down,
her eyes unreading and her mouth all pins.

Page Of First Old Book He Read

I don't know who he is but by his skin
so freckly-pink
    when mine's so worn and fragile
he's new to this, so new he brings me in
    and meets me with his nostrils.

While those two are his eyes his eyes are wells
so brown and deep
    a drop will drop forever
look, this is the dawn of somewhere else,
    his little mouth is opening

an O of sunrise, as if every day
there is to come
    might catch him knowing nothing.
Light will climb with him, time have its say
    when the small voice is ready

and only then, now all the air is breath
until it's quiet.
    Soon his eyes, aligning,
bob along my furrows, tread the earth,
    the ginger head in tow now,

the soft indignant brow becoming clear.
I've bided here
    so long I've quite forgotten
what he encounters, what he's learning there –
    three memories stay with me:

his grin away and back again as if
he'd found somewhere
    we both belonged – slow turning
I took for love – and, when time called enough,
    light narrowing so gently.

Thirty Years

for Derek Walcott

I'm off the phone with Boston and it seems
I'm going there, I'll tell them in a moment.
I'll tell my folks about it, though your name's
unknown to them and new to me. I open
the door to where they're talking
     in our living room in summer

in the nineteen-eighties. – Now it's afternoon.
That Everyman of light is turning helpless
hour by hour, retiring to a den.
Now the call to you, sir, now it's fruitless.
My speckled hand is falling
     towards the blank account-book

to leaf through in the leavings of a Sunday.
Nothing written yet and the clock points.
My reading lamp reflects on the black window
itself alone: no lawn or neighbour's fence,
no trees or distant bedroom
     glow to tilt the mind.

My empty page is a suburban silence,
earnest, available, where nothing goes
at night, here too *there are so many islands*,
mon professeur, and silence I suppose
was pretty much the sound
      I made in our one-to-ones.

Watching as you scanned some early effort.
Retracting it too late as clouds were looked to.
Clouds are looked to now, wish I'd been better,
a better friend, you breathing, me about to,
my heart accelerating
      towards your breaking judgment.

Your empty page was ocean, is still ocean,
lapping the ribs of this. If it's a blank page
anything like mine it sees no reason
to think you won't be back, mistakes the hush
for inhalation, waits
      ecstatically for more.

But it isn't coming in, the light, the heat.
The handle's not about to turn this scene
to us lot sitting where we used to sit,
our ballpoints circling what we think you mean,
our notebooks gaping wide
      on a cold and frosty morning.

Perpetually they wait between the waves,
clear pages yet to come: each one assumes
the turn is coming soon, each one believes
itself the first, like me in that bright room
in Boston, seen clean through,
     man alone with mentor,

turned, what days are for. But nothing turns
now, and nothing breaks. Your own blank page
was ocean, is still ocean going on,
and mine is nothing dining on the edge
of everything. You're there,
     the fixed important jaw,

at the end of a long table, you who were,
pestered by some spectral fans too shy
to say they've *heard* your joke – I haven't, sir,
let's hear it. Look there's nothing of the kind
there at all, but all
     I do in verse these days

is scry the empty page for signs enough.
Love and delight rear up in cliffs and caverns,
forms from Hubble light my heart and home-life,
but on the page? The pure white scrolling heavens,
sod-all else for story
     hereabouts. So help me,

for I knew you for a spell and now you're not,
and my worn hand's still guided like it was
when I was slick. There is a breath in earshot
which isn't always mine, the wince is yours
when the line-break's wrong, the groan
      when I reckon something's finished.

I reckon something's finished, that's my only
reckoning as evening yawns and stretches.
If Everyman was here he wasn't lonely,
for a visitor came by and she stayed ages,
and when they went a book went,
      songs in all its spaces,

a time accounted for. – It's Sunday evening
in a rose-lit living-room, the open arms
of two old chairs, grey cushions, a clock ticking.
I'm off the phone with Boston and it seems
I'm going there, I told them,
      I'm flying in late August,

and there I'll learn my light from dark, my right
delighted scribbling hand from my poor left
there listening one, and how they meet
between the lines, before the weeping crest,
beyond the raging fall –
      or words to that effect –

then I'll come home a fool with a filled book.
Thirty years. The living and the gone
may meet here too, they're here now if you look,
sir, in their shy accord, their one-to-one
that sounds the sound of heartbeats
    pattering through silence.

Small Talk With Time

You ask me what I do
and I say *I've no time for you,*
you make small talk with me,
you make it with eternity.

You ask me am I rude
to everyone and I say *Dude*
you got that straight. You say
you met your perfect match today

you'd like to be together
today, tomorrow, and forever . . .
Then you seem to see
how strange it is you're telling me,

you ask me what I do
and I say *I've no time for you,*
you make small talk with me,
you make it with eternity.

The Heyday

Where is there time for this in a second?
Maybe a spell for a bead of sweat
to be sweat, was it yours is it mine has it happened
    yet? Not yet?

Where is there time for this in a minute?
Nobody's fooled by a minute-hand. Look –
it moves if you look away from it, then it
    moves if you look.

Where's there a window for this in an hour?
There's barely a window for *windows*, except
to let the sun see where we slept, though we barely
    slept where we slept.

Dig me a hole for this in a day-time,
spend Double-Chemistry penning a song –
what *is* the sun but the bell for playtime
    banging on?

Where in the world is the week that's better
than hanging with you? It's not in my iPhone,
not in the Cloud or that Dear John letter
    you sent dear John.

A month? They can rake the moon from a stream
if they think I have time for an Ode to Love
when it's *time* for love – we don't even have time
    for the time we have.

How could I write about this in a year?
the winter will mutter it wasn't like that,
the spring will demur and the summer won't care
    and the autumn lie back

and ponder what time will there be for it all
in a life? And of course being autumn he'll sigh
and he'll write what he writes, as he must, as he will,
    while you and I

are gone like the word, who were more than the word,
whom the word couldn't hold and the word can't see.
The answer to most of my questions is *Nowhere*,
    the rest *Search me*.

The Shudder

With you at work and gone for hours I lay
thinking of you. And in that shade of peace
because I wouldn't dream of it there rose
    to mind some monstrous day

of leaving you, just moving on, grim suitcase
packed, the kitchen thrown a final look,
keys posted through, street gone from, all the work
    of time and trace of us

discarded to one numb rewritten note
you'd notice on a shelf. – I couldn't stand
to have imagined this and wished my mind
    our brimful cat's, all bright

eternally with now. And what was now
got better by the hour – this hideous sight
had somehow softened death, relit its light,
    its circus act, its bow,

compared to what had crossed my mind. I'd seen
a man there never was, could never be –
while death was local, of this parish, he
    and I grew closer then.

Seven Things Wrong With The Love Sonnet

for Anna

Accept this old container from this old
container: *Seven Things Wrong With The Love Sonnet*.
It's planned – we weren't. It's structured to unfold
in a set time – we haven't and we shouldn't.
It lets no silence in – we do and share it.
It boasts it will outlast us – let it try it.
And say it does – we'll not be here to hear it.
And say it doesn't – in our dozing quiet
we shan't miss anything so we shan't miss it.
It's pondering how to end – profoundly sod it.
Sod poetry for its nodding little visit.
For the time it's costing you to have to read it,
for the time it took from me. It's had its say.
Let it stand guard here, say they went thataway.

Waking

When you're
    not here
and leaving blank the page
would say so better than this groan of waking,

before I
    know my
self as stuff at all,
when nothing has transpired, or could, or will

then I'm some
    Adam
fumbling in a wood
made for god-knows-what beyond the word

I have
    for Eve –
the word I have for Eve
is rising to its place – the word I have

is going
    without saying –
now more than sunlight dawns
and more than everywhere and more than finds

the path
    in breath,
whatever comes of it –
should the word *it* mean breath, word, path, or sunlight,

should it
    mean what
makes canvas of the dark,
and, of the desolation, handiwork.

Plainsong Of The Undiscovered

You who go in search
with a lantern and a staff
in the dark that you consider
to be dark that wishes only
    to be scattered by your lantern
may we ask you to remember you are

visible for miles
have been visible to us
from the dark that you consider
to be dark we are observing
    the decisions of your lantern
but what's scribbled by a sparkler wasn't

scribbled there for long
like it wasn't true for long
in the dark that you consider
to be dark we're all around you
    so why don't you shade your lantern
let your aching eyes accustom to the

peace before the thought
in this peace we congregate
from the dark that you consider
to be dark we wish to tell you
    you have no need of a lantern
if you come for us the way we say to

come for us like you
come for us like all of you
for we suffer and we wonder
where we meet we suffer wonder
    we have always been the same
and by that we mean the same as always

changing with the light
and we will not come to light
if you come with black-or-whiteness
do not come with black-or-whiteness
    come with everything between
come with everything there might have been and

bring some who won't come
also some who are long gone
bring the jesting and the yawning
and the reckless and uncaring
    you have been what they have been
come with everyone you never think of

then we'll come to light
or what you consider light
come with every kind of colour
colours you don't think are colours
    colours none of you has seen
we shall be where we have always been and

come for us with love
we say come for us with love
if you do not understànd love
it is dark where you are looking
    we say good luck with your lantern
in a cell that's got no doors or windows

we are leaving now
we may never catch your eye
but we bide and we are hopeful
not for anything just hopeful
    we'll be hopeful if you find us
we'll be hopeful if you never find us

you who go in search
with a lantern and a staff
through the dark that you consider
to be dark we have departed
    and we bless your tiny lantern
from a distance none alive can fathom

Death Comes To Everyman

I hie me to the last-night party
show I'd not played any part in
    hadn't even got around to
catching don't to this day know what
      play it was.

Encounter at the last-night party
jubilant and brimming actors
    watch them reach the end of jokes they
start to ask me what I'd reckoned
      to their show

they're marking with a last-night party
let's derail them with a story
    all about them they don't know I
get them clinking in a dream-world
      gives me time

to sail on through the last-night party
if I might just there excuse me
    you were last to pop the question
in a blue-lit bathroom doorway –
      who are you

what brings you to the last-night party
friend of a friend are you or someone's
    other half were you backstage? – I
raise my phantom glass and cry
      To Theatre!

Advice To The Players

Don't play the ending. You don't know this tale
is written down. You've no idea out there
in shadow shadows watch our long travail,
    some even care, some don't
don't play the ending.

Don't play the ending. Sure you're in Act Five
and five is all you get, the time is short,
whenever you're pretending this is *LIVE*,
    whatever sort of scene
it is it's ending.

Don't play the ending though the players you love
are mostly playing bodies now, effects
have burned the set down and there's not enough
    stage-time left to save
the wretch you're playing.

Don't play the ending though the General's here
for the one line he's been practising, his mask
is pouting on the shelf, don't play the fear,
    don't play the risk you take
don't play what's next

don't play it, though the automatic crowds
who saw the light with one almighty click
are milling in the wings, don't say the words
    the dead have picked for Time
to learn by rote.

Go free, don't play the ending, go free,
as if your final scene is where we meet
at last! with neither prompt nor point nor story,
      beyond a greeting nothing
but the open road,

let's not be fated to, or cursed or blessed
or hinted at, the plot has tried to part us
but the plot is chalked beneath our feet, and dust
      has always let us by
without a word.

Let's not be acted, let's not be rehearsed,
some fool has tried to *mean* with us, let's not
mean, let's turn our backs and do the rest
      out of earshot, eyeline,
out of mind,

Elizabethans then and now, the old crew
finished for the day, in silhouette
beside the river boozing, while the view
      turns gold and lets us go
in our own sweet time.

Thinks It's All There Is

As far as I can see that's everyone.
So thanks for that but where else would you be.
Whatever came or went has come and gone
without you why would you not turn to me.
Look I too turned to me I'm just like you.
Stuff came and went but nothing really took.
So this became what else there was to do.
This became where else there was to look.
This became the language that is spoken
here and here became the only spot.
Here I sense I'm only silence broken.
Here I sing because I see what's not
is almost back. It's frightening, I had plans.
You might have warned me. Hold my hand, both hands —

One Gone Rogue

No one made me, nothing did. I do
get these faces sailing close a while
who seem to see a soul in me like you
and settle their old features to a smile
of all in this together I hate that.
No one made me, nothing did. You can't
meet some stranger over me I'm what
tinder for you what I'm talking point
I'm no one's. Clock me and I clock the fuck
right back at you I've never been begun.
I was never worked on why would I take work
and who would do it? you with the summer gone
and your book in the dead of night you want to try it?
Or me who knows me hasn't it gone quiet.

Love Sonnet Left Behind

Brought to light they say I was by one
the maker wanted with him now. Not now
as in at once but when this work was done.
Which meant he had to pass through me somehow
to get to her was it a her? don't know
my back was turned. The maker was a he
I know for sure though it's so long ago.
A woman didn't make me, look at me.
A woman would have lifted me from this
fixture I was nailed to on that day.
Borne me away and set me down in bliss
somewhere he'll never find me somewhere grey
the many shades of mercy. Somewhere you
who I was made for will be hiding too.

ACKNOWLEDGEMENTS

Some of these poems, or versions of them, first appeared in *Ambit*, *Art & Letters*, the *Guardian*, the *New Yorker*, *Poetry London*, *Poetry Review*, *Sewanee Review*, the *Spectator* and the *Times Literary Supplement*.

'The White' and 'The Heyday' were contributions to *The Voice and The Echo*, in homage to, respectively, George Herbert and John Donne, performed in 2015 in the Sam Wanamaker Theatre at Shakespeare's Globe; 'Pasolini's Satan' was a contribution to an evening of poems inspired by the films of Pier Paulo Pasolini, curated by Simon Barrowclough; 'Song Of Until' was set to music by David Bruce and performed by primary school choirs to celebrate the 25th anniversary of the Voices Foundation; 'Page Of First Old Book He Read' was a contribution to *Off The Shelf: A Celebration of Bookshops in Verse*, edited by Carol Ann Duffy (Picador, 2016); 'Plainsong Of The Undiscovered' arose from *Connections*, a Science and Poetry collaboration with Dr Amber Ruigrok, organized by Lucy Cavendish College, Cambridge.